And God Created "Her"

The Orderliness of God

Rosalyn D. Hickman

Copyright © 2022 Rosalyn D. Hickman
All rights reserved.
No part of this book may be reproduced in any form without permission in writing from the publisher.

Scriptures are taken from the King James Version (KJV).

Published by 4-P Publishing Company
Chattanooga, Tennessee

Edited by Natalie Whalen
Book Cover and Interior Design by Laura Brown
Printed in the United States of America

ISBN- 978-1-941749-18-0

DEDICATED TO...

... all who embrace God's high and holy calling, who delight in revealing God's image and likeness, and who consistently model the *"her"* God created!

... some dear sisters and faithful prayer warriors: Jessica Edwards, Elena Thomas, Brenda Jones, Lacynda Harris, Calister Harris, Denota Fain, Judy Porter, and Tina Burks.

... a beautiful Christian woman and long-time confidant, Marie Pierce: A priceless portrait of a transformed life.

.. Nancy Demoss Wolgemuth, a sister that God brought into my life many years ago through the ministry of Moody Radio. Who because the Holy Spirit clearly revealed a like-mindedness toward God's High and Holy calling for today's woman, we have grown closer over the years.

Contents

Acknowledgments vii

Foreword ix

Introduction 13

The Orderliness of God 25

And God Created Her "Female" 45

And God Created Her "Woman" 63

And God Created Her "Wife" 75

And God Created Her "Mother" 89

Conclusion 101

About the Author 107

Acknowledgments

To my deceased mother, Mrs. Annie Doris Ervin, who was forgiven of much, then fought the good fight, kept the faith, and finished her course: Gladly standing on the Word of God, she was content to leave a legacy of how to live holy in an unholy world.

To my deceased "spiritual mother" Malettor Cross, a faithful missionary and women's speaker who embraced me as her daughter even though she had eleven children of her own.

To all the women who poured the Word of God into me as a child in Sunday School, small group Bible studies, and Baptist Training Union ("BTU") classes.

To faithful men of God, like Manford George Gutzke, Oliver B. Green, and Dr. J. Vernon McGee who, because of my mother's desire to grow in the Word, preached to me the Word of God on radio when there was no "Moody Radio station" in Chattanooga, Tennessee.

Foreword

There are many influences in our culture today. All we have to do is go to the Internet, social media, turn on the television or listen to our friends and family. There are so many opinions out there on every topic. When it comes to women, those voices seem to get louder in regard to defining who we are, our roles, responsibilities and place in life. It can be difficult to distinguish which views are accurate and what direction we should follow based on who says what. We can become confused as to what is right because they can all seem so convincing.

In the beginning of this book, we are directed to see God's specific plan for the "HER" (woman) who is made in His image. As you read these pages, please do not miss the importance of this intentional design. We have God's likeness. Right away, Mrs. Hickman leads us to the fact that we are created beings, male and female, each with a distinct purpose. She points out that we were not designed to compete with one another in our being, but to compliment the other gender. Men and women are made uniquely different for a reason. The author is clear that we are not talking about value or worth in looking at differences between male and female. Galatians 3:28 said regarding our value that "we are all one in Christ Jesus." The scriptures do indicate various roles and responsibilities between genders. This book helps us to see those distinctions and appreciate, not discredit them.

And God Created Her constantly refers us to the Word of God. Scripture is the basis of this book and the ideas in it. While various influences and opinions can taint our view of who we are as women, these chapters constantly take us back to what God says. We are reminded in these pages of Whose image in which we have been created. By being made in the likeness of God, we do not have to succumb to some of the beliefs being screamed at us by our culture. For some of us, we simply need to block out the external noise long enough to personally read the Bible and listen to the direction of the Lord.

The author spent considerable time researching scripture to bring us these thoughts. She then urges us to slow down and do the same for ourselves. We are encouraged to individually delve into God's Word on a regular basis. In doing so, we may see some of the points she is making in a new light. As we look to the Bible for facts

Foreword

regarding being the woman God created, it is quite possible that we will find other guidance He may have for us. Spending quality time in the Word can provide insights, peace, direction and so many other beneficial things for us. It is imperative that we individually study, take notes and pray along the way.

When a concept mentioned here seems contrary to the views of our culture, ask the Lord to show you His way regarding the matter. While some may consider these points to be outdated, we must remember that God is the same yesterday, today and tomorrow and so is His Truth. His Word does not change.

Throughout this book, you may be challenged in the various roles of "HER." While not every reader will find themselves in each of these positions, it is valuable to understand what the Bible says about each of them. Mrs. Hickman does a great job of breaking down the different versions of "Her" that God created. Regardless of where you may find yourself, there are truths to be discovered in considering each of these roles of woman. As you read, look at where scripture may be different from the current views of our world and honestly ask yourself what you believe. Have your thoughts and opinions drifted from God's plan? What adjustments might you need to make to align with His design for you?

These pages provide extensive food for thought. They encourage us to stop and take a deeper look at God's order and how He has called us to live out His likeness in today's culture. As you read *And God Created Her* and ponder these chapters, you may find yourself re-considering some of the voices you allow to influence your thinking. I pray that as a result of reading this book, you will desire to be the "Her" God Created.

Brenda Shuler
Administrator of "Building Lasting Relationships"

Introduction

For many years now, I have had the blessed privilege of teaching and mentoring many young ladies at various stages in both my life and their lives. In fact, it seems as if both mentoring and teaching opportunities found me. As long as I can remember, my love for God and His love for me has encouraged me to embrace the people around me (mainly women and young girls and boys) with their life's concern.

Those joyous times of embracing others sometimes looked like this: Assuring them and explaining that God could help them work through those hard-to-understand situations and tough times; spending quality time with those who just wanted to talk to someone they could trust, and many times helping them resolve disputes by offering peaceful options so they would not give up.

During the process of writing this book, I found many instances where I needed to put my "spin" on concepts to aid in understanding. To separate my thoughts and ideas from the lesson, I have put brackets around these sentences so as to not confuse the reader.

While on this journey, I did not always know the proper name for what I was doing or even recognize where it would all lead. I must confess that at that time, I had never heard the word "mentor," much less knew what it meant. [As I grew older, I realized there were lots of proper terms I didn't know.] Thankfully, knowing proper terms was not a prerequisite for meeting the needs of others. On the other hand, knowing the One who calls and equips us for the tasks in life is what truly matters. As I became more and more knowledgeable of the scriptures, I recognized these mentoring opportunities that I found myself involved in, were discipleship assignments. Some were short-term and others long-term.

Growing up, it seemed I was gripped by the Word of God and its timely messages about holy living. Oddly enough, learning who God was, what He liked and what He didn't like was very attractive to me. Saved at the age of 10, I recognized from the day I asked Jesus to *"come into my heart,"* a real change took place, and I was no longer the same. I knew after listening to that redemption story called the Gospel in the basement/garage of a neighborhood home on Cooley Street, in Chattanooga, Tennessee, that something was wrong with my heart. Those men and women missionaries used a flannel board, which was the visual aid of that day, to illustrate to me and other children close to my age how the red blood flowing from Jesus' side could change my black heart to a white heart. I recognized that day that my heart was the problem and inviting Christ into my heart, where all the evil came from, meant He would change my black heart to a white heart.

Years after God saved me by His Grace, I learned that there is a criticism over the phrase "come into my heart." Some say the statement is not biblical [see what I mean by not knowing proper terms?]. Although the criticism is geared toward those who evangelize using that language, especially with children, it was a bit unnerving for me to hear. But the Holy Spirit immediately comforted me by bringing to my mind the words spoken by the thief who was hanging on the cross to the right of Jesus: *"And he said unto Jesus, Lord, remember me when thou comest into thy kingdom. Jesus replied: Verily I say unto thee: Today shalt thou be with me in paradise." (Luke 23:42-43).* Did God save him? Were his words biblical? Praise God, like that dying thief who cried out and asked Jesus to remember him, I too cried out and asked Jesus to come into my heart. I'm so thankful that the omniscient God knew that both the thief and I were crying out for Him to save us.

Those obedient and caring people first taught us the Gospel and then taught me the truth about my heart! I heard it and I was convicted by the Holy Spirit! I wanted God to save me and change my black heart to a white heart like they showed me on that flannel board. They illustrated the Gospel so a 10-year-old could see it. Looking at it now, I must admit if it is not biblical to invite Jesus into our hearts or tell sinners (children) to invite Jesus into their hearts, at best it genuinely falls under that familiar idiom: **"God knows my heart"**!

Perhaps one way for those who believe the use of these words are unbiblical, is to consider another biblical principal: *"Likewise the Spirit also helpeth our infirmities: For we know not what we should pray for as we ought: but the Spirit itself maketh intercession for us with groanings which cannot be uttered. And He that searcheth the hearts knoweth what is the mind of the Spirit because He maketh intercession for the saints according to the will of God." (Romans 8:26-27)*

Contextually, this reference is encouragement for suffering saints. However, it clearly speaks to a principal of how the Holy Spirit works on our behalf when we don't know what to say. The Holy Spirit not only works on behalf of the saved, but

Introduction

also on behalf of those who evangelize and those who call on the name of the Lord Jesus Christ for salvation who don't know what to say. He searches our heart, and He sees our belief; He sees our repentant heart, and He sees our faith. Even if specific words are not spoken audibly, praise God that the ministry of the Holy Spirit sees and works all of that in and through us at salvation. Take a moment and walk through the scriptures and notice the words that converts and those leading them to salvation use. For example, Saul (Acts 9:6); the Eunuch (Acts 8:36-37); the Roman Jailer (Acts 16:30-32); and the day of Pentecost (Acts 2:37-38, 41).

Consider other scriptures that invite the hurting, the lost, and the weary to cry out to God: *For whosoever shall call upon the name of the Lord shall be saved (Romans 10:13).* And again: *The LORD is nigh unto all them that call upon Him, to all that call upon Him in truth (Psalms 145:18);* and *The sacrifices of God are a broken spirit: a broken and a contrite heart, O God, thou wilt not despise (Psalms 51:17).*

So, maybe what has been called "unbiblical words," lines up more with a cry or a call to God for Salvation. What a comfort, even a relief to know that "Salvation is of the Lord." Sinners and

Christians alike sometimes don't know what we don't know, and we must rely completely on the Holy Spirit to intercede on our behalf with the "right words." My personal prayer concerning this criticism is that the focus and the emphasis would be on the Gospel that is preached and the work of Holy Spirit in Salvation and not the words used when sinners sincerely call upon the Lord. I believe we can all agree that these are not heretical or antibiblical words. Those seeking to win souls for Christ may not totally understand how to break down and explain to unbelievers how the Holy Spirit works in Salvation, nor are they required to. God calls us to go into all the world and preach the Gospel to every creature, but not to perfectly explain or even understand all the workings of salvation [thank God!]. Therefore, some may not always form the perfect phrase for unbelievers to pray. But when we share the Gospel of Jesus "The Christ", He blesses those who answers the call to "Go into all the world and preach the Gospel to every creature."

It wasn't my words that saved me, but it was by *Grace through faith that I believed in Jesus Christ, and He saved me. (Ephesians 2:8-9.)* When those who shared the Gospel with me told me that I was born with a black heart and it needed to be changed to a white heart through the shed blood of Jesus Christ, I asked God to come into my heart and God knew exactly what I meant. He also knew exactly what those who shared the atoning work of Christ with me meant. Praise God He did not turn away from me because of the words, "come into my heart." Thank you, Jesus! The Word of God says the angels rejoice over even one soul that calls upon the Lord for salvation.

    I am so grateful that the Holy Spirit took the words of that little 10-year-old girl [who wanted that "white heart"] and made everything all right. That day she ran all the way home with a note in her hand to give to her mother announcing her salvation! I can still remember the tears of joy that ran down my mother's cheeks as she lay sick in the bed suffering from Lupus, a disease that some years later eventually took her life at the early age of 39. [Ok, I'm about to shout right now so I better move on!]

    Almost sixty years later to-date, I am glad to report that I am just as excited as ever, if not more so, that Jesus saved me and raised me up for such a time as this! Not knowing that the day I asked Jesus Christ to come into my heart, that God would give me so many years to influence other women to receive the work of the Lord Jesus Christ and then to disciple them as they seek to live holy.

Having digressed, let's get back to those things that were attractive to me about God and His Word. Thank God for my mother who valued the Word of God and the wisdom and knowledge she gleaned through the teaching of the Holy Spirit. Because of that, I became a hungry student of the Word of God in my early pre-teen years. Not a scholar, but a student. I wanted to learn all about the God who saved me. I wanted to enjoy the same atmosphere my mother and father created in our home and in our church, and I was able to do just that.

As God directed them, I grew up in Sunday School, Baptist Training Union, morning, and evening worship services and yes, even weekly, small group Bible studies that went from house to house in our very small rural community. In our home, we awoke each morning as my mother prepared breakfast and began her day, to Christian radio. Each program was preaching the Gospel of Jesus Christ with power and conviction while challenging the listeners to be doers of the Word and not just hearers only! I could sense that being a doer was my mom's goal for herself and her children.

Because my mother consistently sought the Lord for her children, I was blessed to participate during my high school years in Bible Quizzing through the ministry of Cedine Bible Camp in Spring City, Tennessee and Campus Crusade for Christ who also had a weekly ministry for teens at my community school, Sale Creek. Bible Quizzing was an exciting, competitive way to hide the Word of God in my heart. Each week missionaries from Cedine and students from Bryan College in nearby Dayton, Tennessee came to my school to engage students in fun and games and a very challenging time in learning the Word!

During those years (1968-70), it seemed the more I heard and learned the scriptures, the more I discovered that everything I needed to know about living out my salvation even in my teen years was in the Bible. Those early years of learning about *"God's Word, His will, His work, and His way"* was foundational to my walk. Learning early in life that a Christian's walk must be based on the truth of scripture and the correct interpretation of the scripture was paramount and foundational. One of those foundational truths I learned was the creation story. That powerful play-by-play story laid out in Genesis 1-2 helped me to understand who God was, how He made me and why He made me! Little did I know that the day would come when this truth would be contested and rejected by so many, even in the "Church"!

This is where we take off! In the first chapter of this book, I point out how the creation story uncovers a correlation between God's order and the *"her"* He created. We explore this correlation in Chapter One, which bears the name of this book's subtitle, *"The Orderliness of God."*

As in my first book, "Anybody Home? In Search of the Titus Woman," may I suggest that you keep a pen and paper handy for notetaking. Take the time to experience those moments when the Spirit of God begins to download in your spirit fresh thoughts and ideas on this subject.

Notes

The Orderliness of God

One attribute about God that has always fascinated me is His orderliness in His person and in His work: I appreciate His *"ways and means"* of operation, if you will.

First, let's look at His orderliness in His work. Simply stated, the way He got things done. No matter how "great" or how "small" the work, God's order was always conspicuous to me. And this fascination with God's order eventually led me to coin the expression, *"The Orderliness of God."*

Notice Moses's description of the earth in Genesis 1. He said the earth was without form, void, and dark. The word "chaotic" comes to mind. But what happened next? We see God, the Holy Spirit who is the third person of the Trinity, move upon the face of the earth and God began to place things into order. Day 1, Day 2, Day 3, and so on. Thus, we see the Triune God bringing order in an orderly fashion. What do I mean by bringing order in an orderly fashion? In His work, we see orderliness in:

- ❖ His approach to creation: He moved, He spoke, He made, and finally, He saw.
- ❖ His arrangement of creation: He designed, He configured, and He organized.

❖ His authority over creation: He named, and He delegated.

What is equally fascinating about God's orderliness in His created work is that it is still as conspicuous today as it was then. The rivers and lakes and bodies of water remain at just the right distance from the land. The sun and the moon still rotate as they were assigned to. The heavens are far above the earth just as God designed them and the seasons of life continue from generation to generation as we experience time. The seconds that make minutes; the minutes that make hours; the hours that make days; the days that make weeks; the weeks that make months and the months that define seasons and establish years. The years eventually inaugurate generations and generations that astoundingly become ages.

Note that all of these are elements of time. And it all happened in succession: sequentially and chronologically. What an Omniscient and Omnipotent God!! Take a few minutes and read through Genesis 1-2. Do you see the three orderly acts of God (His approach, His arrangement, and His authority) in creation? Are you impressed? Are you, in anyway like me, amazed at the orderliness, yet overflowing with curious questions that begin with "why?" For instance, why an All-powerful God took six days to create Heaven and earth? Why, you might ask, did God not just speak everything into existence simultaneously and instantaneously? He very well could have, you know. More questions to ponder:

- ❖ Why did He create man on the 6th day?
- ❖ Why did He make day and night?
- ❖ Why did He make two lights?
- ❖ Why were some things created to live in one environment or atmosphere and others to live in different environment or atmosphere?
- ❖ Why did God make creatures with different shapes and forms?
- ❖ Why were some creatures created to speak words and others to bark or make "weird" sounds?
- ❖ Why do some creatures fly and others crawl?
- ❖ Why didn't God just make everything the same?

Peradventure, there may be theologians, scientists, or extremely serious Bible students who might attempt to answer some of these questions and may even make some mind-blowing points. But, if they did, we would probably be like the little boy who continued to ask his mother "Why?" Even when she thought her every answer would surely be her last answer, he continued to ask "Why?" Soon, the boy's mother wisely responded with a question of her own: "Why not?" she asked. Of course, the boy had no answer, so he quietly moved on. Like this wise mother, instead of trying to answer all the "whys" about God's order, maybe we should ask, "why not" and quietly move on?

The Sovereign God is not obligated to reveal His undisclosed reasons behind His order in creation. In fact, if we are honest with ourselves, our struggle with what God has already "disclosed" to us is enough to keep us busy through all eternity. In fact, "why" questions such as these can distract us from the beauty of what is being revealed about God through His works. Therefore, it is not my intent to explore those stated whys? of creation, but rather to observe and appreciate the order that we see in creation.

As I meditate on Genesis 1, I marvel that the omniscient God revealed through His servant Moses, this amazing creation story. Even though

He knew that the very man He created would, in time, discredit Him as not only "The" Creator but "His" Creator. Yes, the time has come that mankind, like the angel Lucifer, thinks more highly of himself than he ought to think. Even believing that he is a God and that nothing is off limits! He has become so wise in his own eyes that he is convinced that the creation was a result of the "big bang theory." This kind of thinking is an intentional and deliberate strategy of Satan and, has even seeped into some local churches. We understand that world systems are poised to change the rules, the definitions, the order, and even the names of anything that is attached to the only true God and His Holy Word, the Bible.

But I ask, is it possible for a creature to alter the purpose and design of his Creator and make it better? There was a time when a question like this would be viewed as rhetorical and followed by an immediate, resounding, and almost unanimous *"No!"* Of course not! Man could never improve on the work of the Almighty God!

Unfortunately, in this postmodern culture, man would say yes, he can! And even though we know he cannot, he has all but killed for the right to alter and even "redefine" the order of God on so many fronts. Many have even gone so far as to equate such ungodliness as their "civil right." This phenomenon to change God's divine order as we know it is so widespread and seems to be showing up on many fronts in our culture. But looking through the eyes of the Creator who announced that His work was good and very good, these switching of places seem to me to be disrespectful and dishonorable.

But remember, this idea of changing God's order is not a new strategy. It all began in Heaven with the most beautiful angel that I mentioned earlier. His name was Lucifer. He was called "Son of the Morning." *How art thou fallen from Heaven, O Lucifer, son of the morning! How art thou cut down to the ground, which didst weaken the nations! For thou hast said in thine heart, I will ascend into Heaven, I will exalt my throne above the stars of God: I will sit also upon the mount of the congregation, in the sides of the north: I will ascend above the heights of the clouds; I will be like the Most High* (Isaiah 14:12-16).

Now, keep in mind that Satan's strategy has, is, and always will be to parallel the plan of God but with a man-centered evil twist. The strategy begins with self-worship and eventually ends in Satanic worship! Even though Satan knows he is a defeated foe and that he will never be God, he will fight to the very end for that brief moment in time to be worshipped as God by the whole world. He will use all of his deceptive and evil tactics to take center stage and lure mankind away from worshipping the true and living God.

But keep in mind that because God is a God of order, His order even allows Satan, the master deceiver, to roam to and fro seeking to devour whomsoever God allows him to, but only for a season. *"Now there was a day when the sons of God came to present themselves before the LORD, and Satan came also among them. And the LORD said unto Satan, whence comest thou? Then Satan answered the LORD, and said, from going to and fro in the earth, and from walking up and down in it. And the LORD said unto Satan, Hast thou considered my servant Job, that there is none like him in the earth, a perfect and an upright man, one that feareth God, and escheweth evil? Then Satan answered the LORD, and said, Doth Job fear God for naught? Hast not thou made a hedge about him, and about his house, and about all that he hath on every side? Thou hast blessed the work of his hands, and his substance is increased in the land. But put forth thine hand now, and touch all that he hath, and he will curse thee to thy face. And the LORD said unto Satan,*

Behold, all that he hath is in thy power; only upon himself put not forth thine hand. So, Satan went forth from the presence of the LORD." (Job 1:6-12)

To my point concerning God's order, even Satan has to *succumb to God's ways and means of working his evil strategies to steal, kill, and destroy (John 10:10).* God brought up Job's name to Satan. God knew what Satan would do given the chance, and God gave him that chance. It was according to God's plan and order that Satan afflicted Job. [But what and why God ordains evil is another book for another time. Keep looking for it, "THE ODD I SEE (Theodicy)?"]

When God wrote "*Thou shalt have no other gods before me*" (Exodus 20:3), Satan heard it too. I believe Satan immediately resolved to draw man's allegiance away from God and motivate man to worship other gods including other men as well as themselves. Because God has given us a will that is subject to the temptations of the world, the flesh, and the devil, Satan consistently works through our lustful and selfish desires to rearrange, redefine, and remove any semblance of God's original order and replace it with our own. Man has become his own way, truth, and life and is bent on doing what's right in his own eyes.

Have you noticed that man's attitude seems to suggest that God's creation was a good temporary design until a more intelligent people showed up to make things, right? And to man's arrogance, he believes that those "intelligent people" who showed up are right here, right now! What was once considered and presumed ridiculous, even from an unbeliever's perspective, has now become the *"New Normal."* [You will recall I stated in my introduction that I started writing this book 55 years after my salvation. And boy, what a difference 55 years has made in these United States of America.]

A few years back, God's servant, the late Dr. R. C. Sproul and other men of God brought our attention to an amazing doctrine called *"The Otherness of God."* In his message, Dr. Sproul, who passed away since I began writing this book (2018), celebrated the twentieth anniversary of the original release of his book, *"The Holiness of God,"* and looks at *"The Otherness of God."*[1]

As a result, many students of the Bible have since delved into Dr. Sproul's great observation of

---

[1] http://www.ligonier.org/learn/series/holiness-of-god-extended-version/?gclid=CPmU6-ePi8ECFadj7AodDzUAAQ

the *"Otherness of God"* and been reminded that the God of the Bible is not like us or anybody we will ever experience. In this ever-changing world where it seems nothing is like it was, where absolute truth is diminishing day by day, and where "believing" or "not believing" is of no consequence, the true believers are steadfast because of the *"Otherness of God"*! He not only has sanctified us, but He continues to sanctify us day by day. He promised that *what He began in us, He would perform until the day of Jesus Christ (Philippians 1:6).*

In a similar manner, after years of zooming in on the Sovereign God and His marvelous works that we see in scripture, my personal Bible studies have engendered in me a long-time appreciation for God's *orderliness*. Of course, my story leading up to my epiphany of the revelation of the *"Orderliness of God,"* is not as detailed as R. C. Sproul describes his epiphany of the *"Otherness of God."* However, my momentous experience is so etched in my spirit and revered in my heart that I literally see God's order in my study-times even though I'm not looking for it.

Although these two expressions have a similar ring, I am in no way claiming that the two are equal in printed theological writings or studies by mainstream Bible scholars of today or in the past. I never thought about Pastor Sproul's title, *"The Otherness of God"* until I wrote down my words in my Bible study notes. Those words were my placeholder for my following day's study. It was a common practice of mine to make up headings for places to begin on the next day or next Bible study time. That day in 2012, was when it dawned on me the similarity of the two expressions. Of course, it's bound to happen when the same Holy Spirit is doing the teaching from the same inspired Word of God about the same God!

For me, at times, it seems as though God's order is the theme of the entire Bible. So, I invite you to quote me as I pen this expression that originated from my close observation of that God-breathed text: *"So God created man in his own image, in the image of God created he him; male and female created he them."* (Genesis 1:27)

Here's how this phrase evolved in my studies: For years my husband Gary and I have taught marriage classes, provided complimentary marital and premarital counseling to many couples, and spoken at conferences, retreats, and numerous workshops. So, it stands to reason that for many years we have referenced and unpacked, to the best of our abilities, what God would have us to teach from His Word for couples to model Christ and the church in their marriages. We have always been careful to point each audience to the appropriate scriptures and cross references that pertained to God's ordained roles and responsibilities as well as our complimentary male/female differences.

Long before our organized couple-to-couple ministry, Covenant Keypers, Inc., I often referred to God's order when mentoring or teaching women about the role God created. Looking back, I realize that I was developing a passion for what unfortunately today has become a very controversial issue, even among Christian women. That controversy, as I see it, is primarily centered around God's order for women submitting to those in authority over her, whether in the home, in the church or life in general.

However, my passion and my desire to practice biblical submission was born out of observing my mother's attitude and practice of submission in the home. After two failed marriages, her desire to love, honor, and obey her third and final husband (my stepfather) became my model. Not because he was so deserving necessarily, but because she now understood that to love, honor, and obey her husband was to love, honor and obey God. Loving, honoring and obeying God was an automatic link to her marriage relationship with her husband. I can honestly say that my mother's teaching by example made sense to me even then. Please don't understand me to say that my mother and father had a perfect and trouble-free marriage. They didn't! But what I know is that they knew and embraced God's order and was very intentional in their application. I'm sure my dad would have much rather been in my mom's place than to be in the role that God ordained for him to love his wife as Christ loved the Church. How huge is that!? But when we think about it, all of God's commands are huge, right?

So, as a teenager growing up in a home where the Word of God was so pronounced and seemed to work to the glory of God, I was convinced after 6th grade that God's order was the better way to go. What was obvious was that in my mother's previous marriages, it was not that way. Although I was very, very, young, I was not too young to know that I never wanted what I saw and heard in those previous marriage relationships! After witnessing all the arguments, physical abuse, the nightclubbing, and the anxieties that came with those earlier marriages, it was no wonder my desire was to model what I witnessed in my mother's last marriage. I was sold on God's order. For me, it translated as peace. Peace in the home, peace in the church, and more important peace in me. Only God's order brings about peace!

As I grew older in Christ, you might say I became somewhat of a cheerleader for God's order. Not just in marriage, but in all of life. Even today as I disciple women, I begin with "Who is God?" which takes off in Genesis and I share with them His person and His work! Honestly, the more I cling to God's order and reject the world's order, the more I'm motivated to encourage other sisters to do the same.

Declaring in no uncertain terms, this is not the time for shrinking back, but for moving forward! As women of faith, we must not buy into the world's absurd and erroneous views about God's order for women. We must stand firm on the fact that we have been created to pursue holiness and to glorify God. What a great time to *"Hold forth the Word of life; that we may rejoice in the day of Christ, that we have not run in vain, neither labored in vain."* (Philippians 2:16)

Of course, the enemies of Christ (the flesh, the world, and the devil) are working harmoniously and intentionally to steal, kill, and destroy God's order on every front. Satan knows that he was defeated at Calvary; nevertheless, he will not give up until he has deceived as many as he can, including the women and the children. Satan is a powerful force to reckon with and has a notable history of warring against God and His order. Remember his uprising in Heaven and how one-third of the angels were cast down with him when God cast him out of Heaven? Remember too that his first successful battle on earth was with the woman? And even though God cursed him to crawl on his belly and eat the dust of the earth, he is still no less determined to thwart the plan and order of God.

Notwithstanding, God's mandate for the older women to teach the younger women is still on the table. It's not a suggestion or something God is strongly recommending. It is a mandate that God has entrusted primarily to the women of God to teach and to model. In so doing, God's image and likeness will be reflected throughout the whole world just as He intended. And that is why God's order for the roles and responsibilities of women will continue to clash with the world's order. Thus, we have that unbiblical but persistent battle between the sexes!

That mandate in Titus 2:4-5 to teach the younger women to be sober, to love their husbands, to love their children, to be discreet, to be chaste, to be keepers at home, to be good, and to be obedient to their own husbands is a very stern yet affectionate message that flows directly from the heart of the Creator through the Apostle Paul. As clear and simple as the message is, it can be ambiguous to the natural woman and sometimes viewed as controversial to say the least. To reference the words of our 2014 Church Leadership Conference speaker, Dr. Steven Lawson, *"God's Word is not hard to understand, it's just hard to swallow!"* But knowing that God's order is far better than ours: *"We will do well to swallow it and live soberly, righteously, and godly in this present evil world. That is what the Grace of God will teach us to do."* (Titus 2:11-12).

These are a few of my deliberations that led to my epiphany, *The Orderliness of God*. I could no longer deny that what I had experienced in my walk with God was a truism that God is indeed a *"God of Order"* and it is seen in His person and His work.

With that in mind, let's proceed and survey some of my personal interpretations/observations of the *"her"* God created and how these seem to underline the *Orderliness of God*. I say "personal," because these were some of the things that jumped out at me as I meditated on God's orderliness in creation.

Let me say right up front that I am not purporting any biblical interpretations, suggesting any doctrinal or theological positions, with these observations: Quite the contrary. Rather, the point of this book, as with my life, is simply to reason with today's Christian women concerning who we are in Christ and some biblical motivations to inspire us as we: *"work out our salvation with fear and trembling."* (Philippians 2:12)

We begin with the first of the four identities of the *"Her"* God created: "The Female."

Notes

And God Created Her "Female"

(Different)

The Book of Genesis is categorically acknowledged as the "Book of Beginnings." One might even argue that everything that came to be had its origin in those first 50 chapters of the Bible. The remaining 1,139 chapters build on those. You might even identify with me in this: Whenever I'm curious about a word, a principle, or a teaching, I find myself revisiting those first 50 chapters of Genesis to find its first reference and gain a better understanding of a later text. I suspect this practice is certainly not unique to me. If you are an inquisitive Bible student, more than likely you have a similar practice.

In the first four chapters of Genesis, we see the first four distinct identities of the *"Her"* that God created revealed. Based on my observations of scripture, I see all of her other identities flowing from these four. As we look at each of her identities, notice how each draws attention to the *"Orderliness of God."*

As we began, I confess that, in my humble opinion, except for the birth and the crucifixion of Jesus Christ, the creation is the most captivating story in the entire Bible. Because it is so captivating, it is quite possible to read through this entire

"Female"

story and miss the unveiling of the four *"her"* identities God created, although they unfold right before our eyes. For sure, by the end of the third chapter of Genesis, one would not only have seen her four identities, but also; 1) seen how the Triune God-like orderliness correlates to her design, her roles, and her responsibilities; and 2) how those unique roles and responsibilities correlate to the unique roles and responsibilities of the *"him"* God created *(Adam)*.

Before I wrote this chapter, I will admit that I discovered some interesting writings about the syllable "fe" in the name female, and I almost included some of those findings in this chapter, but wisdom said no. Mainly because I find it more fruitful to write about the things seen and revealed in the scriptures on this subject. And although interesting, I found no clear biblical support for those writings. That was enough for me to say no.

So, here we go, *The Female*. I discussed earlier that my first attraction to the *"Orderliness of God"* was seen in *His work* (the creation of everything.)

Now we come to Genesis 1:26 which states in part: *And God said, let us make man in our image, after our likeness:...."* Following that, Genesis 1:27 states: *So, God created man in His own image, in the image of*

God created he him; male and female created He them. It was these two verses that I saw the orderliness of *His person!*

This is the first time during the creation, God acknowledges with His own words that there were others with Him participating in the creation. He spoke the words, "us" and "our." The Bible argues that these pronouns actually describe the plurality of the Godhead and is confirmed in other scripture passages. One such passage is found in the Apostle John's gospel: *In the beginning was the Word, and the Word was with God, and the Word was God.* (John 1:1) *Other* supporting scriptures of the Triune God are John 14:10-11; 16:13; and 17:21-22.

Not only is God unfolding the plurality of the persons in the Godhead but the relationship, the role, and the function of the Godhead; three but one. Notice the word, "us." Obviously, "us" implies more than one person. Next, the words: "our image and our likeness" underscores the sameness and the distinctions of the Godhead. And finally, the words: "make man" expresses the role and function of the Godhead in creation. Because Moses records the words, *"then God said let us,"* we believe this conversation was between God the

Father, God the Son, and God the Holy Spirit. Very much like the conversation Jesus has with His Father in John 17 in the Garden of Gethsemane.

Let's be sure to note that no other creature was made in God's image or likeness. As much as we love our pets and try to humanize them, there is no other creature made in the image and likeness of God. This is a part of that phenomenon we mentioned earlier about man switching God's order.

So, when God said: "Let us make man in our own image and likeness," I looked intently at what Moses had identified and revealed up to that point about His image and likeness. What did we really know then about His image and likeness when God made that statement? Was there enough revealed after the creation of man in the book of Genesis to clearly see God's image and likeness? Or maybe we could fast forward through the scriptures and continue to corroborate and support the fact that man was indeed created in the image and likeness of God. I'm sure the latter is true, but keep in mind that the former is the very point of "And God Created Her" in the *"Orderliness of God."* I believe enough is in the book of

Genesis to clearly see the image and likeness of God in the *"her"* God created.

On that premise, let's continue: My intent to look at God for clues about His image and likeness could only be derived from the text up to that point. What had I seen? As my Pastor Eddie D. Jacks, often says, ".. . it's in the text!" I saw His person and His work. Moses revealed His name and His work to the readers in the first four words in the Bible. What a *subtle* yet obvious introduction. Subtle in that you can just read right through it and not realize the orderliness being reflected in the word "God," yet, <u>obvious</u> in that no one can deny His name is God. I then thought there might be something about His image and likeness reflected in God's name and *"her"* name *(female)*. Moses says this: *"So God created man in His <u>own</u> image; in the image of God created he him; male and female created He them."* Genesis 1:27 (KJV). What is in the identity of a female that reveals God's image and likeness? I rehearsed over and over the words God used in verse 26: "in <u>our</u> image and after <u>our</u> likeness." As I began to meditate, I recalled the name God is plural and is the exact expression of the Trinity sometimes referred to as the Godhead, or the Triune God: *God the Father, God the Son, and*

God the Holy Spirit.

As intriguing as the Godhead is, I will refrain from having a theological discussion on that mind-blowing doctrine, although I am tempted to go down that path. Keep in mind as you read, my goal is to simply identify the image and likeness of God that we see in the *"her"* God created and subsequently appreciate His orderliness.

Recognizing how both the Triune God and the male and female shared one another's names respectively, I paused. There it was staring me in the face. The Godhead shares the name "God," and the male and female shares the name "male." In our next chapter we will see how that sharing of names is also reflected in the second identity: "man and woman." The Godhead is one in essence (co-equal) and yet three unique, separate, and distinct persons and so is the male and female He created. Not only does the identity of male and female reflect the image of God the Father, God the Son and God the Holy Spirit, but it reflects His likeness and His order.

Many years ago, while studying the creation of male and female, this word screamed from the pages of my study that morning! "Different." That's what I saw. I quickly began to incorporate this teaching in my workshops, seminars, and retreats. I felt an urgency to create a biblical understanding in the hearts of the women I spoke to and prayed that they would embrace the identity of male and female as different as seen in the Godhead!

Of course, as I mentioned earlier, they were one in essence, but remember the plurality? So how do I reconcile two terms that on the onset sound contradictory? So, here's the phrase the Holy Spirit taught me as I intently looked at the text: *"Complimentary Differences."*

I coined the phrase "complimentary differences" because it best articulates and authenticates the congruency of the names male and female in the same way the name *"God,"* articulates and authenticates the congruency of the names in the Godhead: God the Father, God the Son, and God the Holy Spirit. On the one hand, all share the same name and on the other hand, all have distinct names.

Let me quickly add that the name female in no way indicates competition any more than the name God in the Godhead indicates competition. Quite the contrary! This first identity I observed in the *"her"* God created, simply reveals, right out the gate, that even her gender as female is indicative of God's image and likeness. God's image is seen in her shared name "male" and God's likeness is seen in her different name "female." Now compare it with "God," the shared name in the Trinity; and "The Son," the different name in the Trinity. The different name is the unique identifier.

Maybe a better way to think about it would be, differences that compliment. Her complimentary differences can be summed up in one word: Gender! We understand the female gender is at the root of the greatest compliment that the male will ever experience in this life. Even to her physical sexual part, she is different and yet complimentary. She is physiologically poised in her body to receive and respond to the male who is physiologically poised in his body to initiate and lead. I'll go out on a limb to say that this coined phrase, *"Complementary Differences"* is at the root of what links the remaining three identities to the image and likeness of God that otherwise we would never realize. I strongly believe the differences are a key component to what leads to the deepest moments of intimacy that can ever be experienced on earth between the male and the female, namely sex; in particular through the role of a husband and a wife. We will discuss in detail just how deep this intimacy really goes when we look at God's beautiful design for sexual intercourse between husband and wife! Stay tuned.

So, from the greater to the lesser, I saw God's image and likeness in the name *"female."* He made the female *"like"* the male, but *"different"* from the male: Just as the Godhead is equal but distinctly different from one another. Of course, their names will speak to their work as we will see the scripture unfold before our eyes in the remaining chapters of this book.

Another point about the image and likeness of God seen in the name female is the order that these names are verbally expressed and written. These names are revealed in a particular and intentional order, and it is very difficult for me to believe that it is a coincidence. There are no coincidences with God! My friend Ron Jones refers to these kinds of happenings as *"Godcidents"*. Moses, the writer of Genesis, is not oblivious to name "God." Moses knew the Hebrew word for God was Elohim which is the plural form of *"El"* sometimes translated as "gods."

So, when Moses opens the book of Genesis

with *"In the beginning God,"* it was not an accident. Moses knew all too well the God who said, *"Let us make man in our image, in our likeness...."*. He sheds light on this community of the Godhead right off the bat. I can't say emphatically that Moses knew that the us was God the Father, Son and Holy Spirit but as God breathed on the writers of scripture to write, it would not surprise me what God revealed to Moses about Himself. We know that in this Godhead, God is the head of Christ although Jesus and the Father are one. John 17, I Corinthians 11:5. And because he is the Father, we reference them as God the Father and God the Son and not God the Son and God the Father. You might think to mention such references is insignificant or maybe even unnecessary; but obviously I begged to differ. Remember, Moses introduces Him to us as *"In the beginning God"*.

In like manner, the way we reference the female is also in the order she was introduced to us by Moses. We rightly reference them in order of their creation male and female. Birth order has a significance throughout the book of Genesis and the entire Bible as we eventually learned. Again, that is no accident—equal but different. We see Him revealed throughout the scriptures as God the Father, God the Son, and God the Holy Spirit. As well, that same order is seen throughout scriptures for male and female. From Genesis to Revelation, you will never see or hear any reference to the Godhead spoken in some flighty or precarious order, i.e., God the Son, God the Holy Spirit, and God the Father or any other variation. Nor will you ever see the scriptures reference the genders as woman and man, female and male, wife, and husband. That is again because we are His likeness, and we reflect His likeness automatically and without pause. But hear me when I say, the time is coming when this too will be another target of the enemies of Christ to dismantle!

The relationship between the Godhead is all about the orderliness of God and so is the relationship between the male and female. Don't get it twisted: The order of His spoken name and the order of *her* spoken name is intentional and should not be ignored or irreverently distorted. To do so would be a misrepresentation of His image and likeness. God's standard for order is born out of who He is. He is a God of order. It is just like God to reflect His Sovereignty even in the order of His name. If you will allow me, I coined that observation of God's name as "God's heavenly hierarchy."

Buried within the name Father, Son, and Holy Spirit; and Male and Female, are other elements that point to the specific relationship, role, and responsibility of the Godhead and the *"her"* He created for His own glory. We will continue to explore those elements as we unveil the last three identities of the *"her"* God created.

A Sidenote for Emphasis on Man's Attempt to Switch Places

For years, I've respected and appreciated these discoveries and felt they warranted considerable attention by other women. However, I'm well aware that this is not a welcomed world view of today's females inside or outside the Christian Church. It is not something they embrace as "complementary."

Here's the progression God opened my eyes to about today's culture. By just consistently and systematically studying God's Word and watching and listening to what was happening around me, I noticed three things that were very disquieting. And this is my summary statement I usually open with when addressing this topic of today's discontented female.

Number one: I noticed how many women

deny the male and female distinctions under the disguise of equality. This is often associated with and aligned with "The Women's Liberation Movement." The emphasis on men vs. women is almost an obsession with many women and seem to carry an argumentative tone. Even though I was a young professional wife at the time, I thought the focus of **being equal to the man** was a bit excessive and, in some way, suspicious.

The next thing I noticed was how that emphasis segued right into their next big push, that somehow now **"women were better than men."** Competition was the new conversation, and the "battle of the sexes" heightened. Battles were showing up everywhere. From game shows to sports events. You could feel the competition taking on a real attempt to prove that women were smarter, faster, and stronger than men.

As time progressed, this competition between the sexes and advanced onto many fronts. Traditional roles where men dominated were being challenged by women everywhere: in education, sports, politics, church, social clubs, pubs/bars, and yes even aeronautics, etc. Wherever there seem to be exclusivity for the man, the females' underlying goal was to prove that females are

"Female"

equal to and better than the man and should be viewed, included, and accepted as such everywhere.

And finally, I see that the woman's agenda is to literally become a man physically! To that end, she now plays the role as man in the sexual lesbian relationship. She changes her body through surgical procedures to eliminate her female birth body parts. How wicked is that? Roman 1:26.

The enemy is so shrewd and so cunning that he has moved women into the very place that most resembles him! His covetous spirit, his evil character, and his determination to steal, kill and destroy. Remember, all that God has made, Satan wants to eliminate or remake, especially the male female who He created in His image and likeness. From the beginning, Satan has always wanted to be God. When he said I will be "like" the Most High, he meant "I will be the Most High."

We see an out and out move on the part of women to become a man. From cross-dressing to sex change operations, you name it, we're there. Homosexuality and lesbianism are just another form of rejecting the male/female differences we discussed in this chapter. And so, it is safe to say that the last three identities that God created her to be, will also be the target for this culture to deny, reject, and ultimately attempt to recreate. The scary part is that the "deceived church-goers" seem to be right on board! But hold on, we will unpack all of that in our upcoming chapters.

One last thought on the female God created in his image before I close this chapter. Notice how females today seek their identity from popular and famous celebrities and successful entertainers. How unfortunate it is they would carelessly overlook God the Creator and seek their identity from other created mortals.

Of course, watching all the efforts made by women past and present have taken me aback given what I understand about the creation story. There is no question that recognizing and focusing on the image and likeness of God in us has been far better for me. So, as you reflect and meditate on this first unveiling of the "her" God created, my prayer is that you will be content in being female even more.

"Female"

Notes

And God Created Her "Woman"

(Relationship)

Now let's zoom into scripture and discover the next *"her"* that I observed in the creation story. It is an observation that is familiar to all of us. Let's look at the first time we see the identity of the "woman" disclosed in scripture. As I said before, I am referring to the first time it is seen in the King James Version of the Bible. I'm not sure if all versions have kept the same progression in their translations. My prayer is that there is no change in the timelines of creation in other versions of the Bible.

In Genesis 1:28, we see the first time we see her identity called "Woman"! God never designed Adam to be alone. Eve was always in the heart of God. Even before God said, "Let us make man in our image and after our likeness," He had both Adam and Eve in mind. Like the animals, Adam was designed to have a suitable helper. A helper that was also created in the image and after the likeness of God. The "woman" God created, not unlike the "female" that God created, was also a picture of the Trinity. The image and likeness of the identity of the male and female manifest their complimentary differences. However, the image and likeness of the name man and woman manifest their relationship to one another. Again, we see in both their names man and woman the word, "man." But this time, it denotes "relationship." Just as the word God in the Godhead denotes their relationship: God the Father, God the Son, and God the Holy Ghost. Each is God. Not three gods. One God, three persons! In that likeness, the man and the woman are one: One man, two persons. Remember how Eve arrived? It was through an extraction from the man's side. His very person was invaded through what we call surgery or an operation. From that person, God built or formed another person and Adam is no longer by himself. What was in the beginning one person is now two persons. The man, and then the woman. Her identity as woman was explained at the time Adam named her. He explained, she would be called woman because she was taken from him, "bone of my bone and flesh of my flesh."

How pertinent was this statement? "Bone of my bone and flesh of my flesh"? Why did God pull the bone or the rib from Adam's side to make the woman? Why didn't He pull a kidney or pull from the heart or brain? What is the significance of the bone and the flesh?

When we say that the Father and the Son and the Holy Ghost are one in essence, but three persons, what does essence intimate? The answers to these questions will simultaneously reveal the woman's image and likeness of God's order of God. We will also once again witness God's order in the creation of the woman.

So, what is being communicated when we say the Father, Son, and Holy Spirit are one in essence, but three in persons? First, let's look at two other scriptures that address the essence and position of the woman in creation:

> *For the man is not of the woman, but the woman of the man. Neither was the man created for the woman but the woman for the man.*
> *(I Corinthians 11:8-9)*

> *But I suffer not a woman to teach, nor to usurp authority over the man, but to be in silence. (Why?) For Adam was first formed, then Eve.*
> *(I Timothy 5:12-13)*

Can you see the essence in the words; *the woman is "of the man"?* Clearly, she was not created from the dust or from any other creature. She is of the same man God created with his own hands! In I Timothy 5:13, we see Paul referencing the order of her creation as seen in the book of Genesis when he reminds us that Adam was created first then Eve. We will see in the next chapter how the order of her creation ties to her next identity. In the meantime, remember the implication I linked to the word *woman* is "relationship." Every identity of the *"her"* reveals an aspect of God's image and likeness and subsequently, His orderliness. In the same way there is a relationship in the Godhead in essence, there is also a relationship in the person of the man and the woman. Let's look at the essence of God through the writings of Dr. Charles Coppens.

Dr. Charles Coppens of the University of Notre Dame says this concerning the essence of God[2]:

Chapter II; The Essence of God.
"The essence of a thing is that which constitutes it intrinsically, making it what it is; it is the note or notes without which a thing can neither exist nor be conceived." ". . . That the nature of God is not divisible; and therefore that, once we learn by Revelation that there are three distinct Persons in God, we know that they must have the same individual nature: nor can there be a real

---

[2] https://www3.nd.edu/~maritain/jmc/etext/lamp25.htm

distinction between the nature of God and the Persons, but only between the Person as such, so that the Father is not the Son, and yet He is the same being as the Son."

Coppens further writes:

Article I. Physical and Metaphysical Essence Of God.

229. The physical essence is the essence viewed exactly as it is in the being itself, not introducing into it such distinction as do not belong to it in the objective reality. Now, there are no real distinctions in the essence of God, as we shall show further on, therefore His physical essence is simply the sum total of His perfection.

230. But the metaphysical or notional essence of a being is its essence as conceived by us, i.e., as it is traced out by our mind, and marked out in different perfections with logical distinctions, which are not objectively real, though they have a foundation in the reality. The metaphysical essence is viewed as distinguished from the attributes, and, in a created being, as distinguished from the accidents. In God there are no accidents; for He necessarily is all that He is.

Now, the essence as distinct from the attributes is

conceived as, (a) so proper to a being as to distinguish it from every other being, and (b) so primary that all the attributes flow from it."

So, without making what is already a very difficult concept to understand more difficult, simply put, the woman God created shares God's likeness in how she relates to the man. The man and the woman relate to one another in essence. No other creature equates in any way with the man and woman in essence [although modern man's inordinate affection for animals is leaning more and more toward a disregard to that uniqueness]. Both the man and woman relate perfectly even in their imperfections. The creature that Adam called *"woman"* can never cease to be his kind in essence, any more than the Father, the Son and the Holy Spirit can cease to be God. So, while continuing my gaze into the text, I observed how the *"woman"* relates to the person of the man as the persons in the Godhead relate to one another.

Isn't it beautiful when we pause and give attention to the Word of God? When He said: "in our image and likeness," He did just that. He clearly shaped, designed, and fashioned us in His image and likeness. So far, we've observed it in our "female-ness" and our "woman-ess." And what a blessing it is to be created in the image and likeness of the all-powerful, all-knowing, everywhere at-the-same-time God! Are you thinking along with me as I share my observations? What images and likenesses are you realizing about the *"her"* God created?

Only when we slow down and reflect on God's Imago De' can we begin to appreciate the *"her"* we really are. And the more we learn about the Triune God, the more amazed we might be at how special we must be to God. That He would bestow such an honor on us speaks to the love He has for mankind. We see His love continuing to play out with the calling of Abraham, whom we know as *"a Friend of God."* Just think, the image and likeness that we experience now is only a preview for when we see our Creator face to face. We can only imagine what it will be like *"to know even as also we are known"* (I Corinthians 13:12).

When our observation of the Godhead deepens, the image and likeness of the woman begins to make more sense, beginning with her desire to marry. Like the trinity, there is a unique and natural attribute in a woman to connect with the man in an "us" kind of way. This desire to connect is mutual. Again, it is like no other earthly connection. This disposition for the woman to connect with man whether in marriage or in pre-marital or even casual relationships comes from God. At the risk of repeating myself, these relationships are natural because it's her essence that is being reflected. Although different as we addressed in the previous chapter, it is indicative of the woman (and the man) to build meaningful relationships and pursue life with a semblance of unity and being of the same mind and on one accord. The words *"let us"* and *"our image and likeness"* speaks to the unity and same mind in the Godhead. Although challenging for the woman (and the man), to live out that unity perfectly, it is non the less an undeniable likeness of God being experienced. It is most powerful to the woman (and man) and glorifying to God.

Another obvious image and likeness of God in the *"woman He created"* is her desire to relate through conversation. In short, women like the Godhead enjoy and revel in the communion that comes with relationships. Of course, we've heard all the statistics that accuse women of talking more than men. However, having seriously observed the Godhead, we can now better understand where our natural tendency to talk comes from. Where else? The image and likeness of God!

Does this sound familiar? In the beginning was the Word and the Word was with God and the Word was God. Ok, that makes sense. One can always observe the Godhead communicating with the other beginning in Genesis all the way through Revelation. Many times, Jesus would steal away to pray to His Father early in the morning while here on earth. Remember His prayer in the Garden of Gethsemane? In that prayer remember how Jesus was longing to be with his Father. He referred to the time when they were together in the beginning. And finally, on the cross as He was dying, just before He gave up the ghost, He talked with His Father. It was a terrible time when God had to turn His back on His Son. To hear Jesus cry out "My God, My God, why has thou forsaken me" was a very dark day in the life of Jesus. But you know why He did it? For His children that He called, elected, and justified before the foundation of the world.

Not only does the Godhead talk with one another but God has also been communicating with man since He created him and placed him in the Garden of Eden. He often visited with Adam and Eve in the cool of the day to communicate with them (Genesis 3:8). Sufficeth to say, we have 65 more books in the Bible of conversation between God and man. Before Jesus came to earth, God often spoke to man in various ways and means.

The Book of Hebrews highlights God's means of communicating with man in sundry times through his leaders like Moses, through the Law, angles, priests, prophets, prophetess, kings, apostles. Then in the fullness of time, He sent his only begotten Son to commune with man for 33 years. Finally, He sent the Holy Spirit who today speaks on His behalf through his Word. It's no wonder the woman takes full advantage of the interfacing and interaction of communication especially in marriage. It's her image and likeness of God coming through. More on that in the next chapter.

In summary, my two observations of the *woman* God created is all about how her relationship and communication with the man reflects that of the Godhead. Do you see His Person and Work on display?

In the next chapter we will see how the design for the man and woman to connect intimately was fulfilled when God created her *WIFE*.

Notes

And God Created Her "Wife"

(Her Role)

So, what is it about the *wife* that reflects the image and likeness of God? How is God's order on display in the wife? Before I answer that question, let's see what's revealed in the text.

Notice that before God ever made the woman, He identified a need in the man (Adam) and described what her role would be. He clearly stated: *"It is not good that the man should be alone; I will make him a help meet for him."* (Genesis 1:28). But don't get it twisted; Adam was not alone in the Garden as in "without company or living in a solitary place." Adam had fellowship with God the Father, the Son, and the Holy Spirit. He was surrounded by the beasts and creeping things on the earth, fish in the sea, and fowls in the air. So, in no way was he lonely. So, let's look carefully at this idea of a help meet for the man.

According to God, Adam was created with an intentional missing counterpart. But the missing counterpart was inside him. To borrow an illustration from our friend and pastor, Roger Skepple, Pastor of Berean Bible Baptist Church in Atlanta, GA, who noticed this: *Just like the ground had a problem and the solution was inside the ground, (Genesis 2:5-7)* which was the man; likewise,

Adam's solution was inside him. God put Adam to sleep and pulled from him a help meet that would cure his being alone. No longer would Adam be without the help he needed to carry out God's work. In fact, when God gave Adam his first job, (naming the animals), God knew Adam would discover what He already knew: That Adam was alone and needed a help meet. After naming all the animals, Adam would have a desire to have what the animals had, a help meet not like their kind but his own kind which was God's image and likeness.

He saw more than the complimentary differences of male and female that we talked about in the Female chapter; he saw more than the relationship between the woman and the man we discussed in the Woman chapter; he saw her unique role to and for him as he named those animals.

At this point, let me mention this to the single men and women who may be reading this book: About the orderliness of God, it's noteworthy to mention that Adam had a job and a home before he had a wife and in our next chapter, we will see that Adam and Eve were married before they had children. So, please note God's order when reading the Word of God. Not only were families ordained by God, but the timely order of families was also ordained by God.

Now when God said Adam was alone, we now know what God meant. Adam needed a wife. Someone to *help him carry out God's commandments (Genesis 2:16),* to dress and keep the Garden; and Genesis 1:28, to be fruitful, and multiply, and replenish the earth, and subdue it; and have dominion over the fish of the sea, and over the fowl of the air, and over every living thing that moveth upon the earth. None of the other creatures could be Adam's helper because they were made after their own kind. They were not made in the image and likeness of God. God always knew Adam needed someone different from him but someone like him: Someone who was his essence but not his person. Sound familiar? With that, let's see how the wife reveals the image and likeness of the Triune God?

I intentionally focused on the phrase "help meet" and it popped out to me immediately. The image and likeness that God revealed in the wife was the Holy Spirit: The third person of the Trinity. Did you see it? Helper, Help Meet?

Let's explore the first time we see the Holy Spirit at work. To do this, let's look at Genesis, Chapter 1.

When Moses introduced us to a world not yet

formed and full of darkness and chaos, we saw these words: *And the earth was without form, and void; and darkness was upon the face of the deep. And the Spirit of God moved upon the face of the waters.* (Genesis 1:2)

Notice, the Godhead spoke, and the Spirit moved. Right from the beginning we see the Spirit functioning respective to His person: Moving, helping, assisting, enabling. The scripture clearly reveals the Spirit in this light. Phrases like: *"moved on," "came upon," "moved through," "moved in,"* and *"moved by"* are often used or implied when the Spirit worked in people or situations. One example was when Jesus explained being born again to Nicodemus, He distinctly linked the wind to the Holy Spirit.

The wind bloweth where it listeth, and thou hearest the sound thereof, but canst not tell whence it cometh, and whither it goeth: so is everyone that is born of the Spirit. John 3:8

Often, we see the Holy Spirit exerting force in some manner. That is probably why He is sometimes innocently referred to as an "it" by uninformed and/or new Christians. An example of force is seen in phrases like: *"Baptized by the Spirit," "the Spirit like a rushing mighty wind," "the Spirit helps our infirmities," "Walk in the Spirit," "Filled with the*

Holy Spirit, they began to speak," "As the Spirit gave them utterance," etc.

These all speak to the function and role of the Holy Spirit in the Godhead. In the same way, the wife also brings movement, power and force to her husband just as God designed her to. She is empowered with a force that is readily seen in her respective role to her husband in marriage. What exactly am I talking about? Well, let's allow the scriptures to speak again.

A clear way to understand the action and movement of the wife in the marriage relationship is to look at some examples in scripture. Let's look at Adam and Eve. When Adam knew his wife (engaged in sexual intimacy with her), she brought forth two sons: Cain and Able; when Abraham entertained the angels who came to destroy Sodom and Gomorrah, at Abraham's directions, it was Sarah, his wife, who cooked the meal for them; when Nabal refused to feed David and his men, it was his wife, Abigail, who made it happen and kept David from killing Nabal; when Elijah was hungry, it was the wife, now widow of Zarephath who prepared the meals each day; when the Proverb's wife's husband and children needed clothing, it was the well-known Proverb's woman who stayed up late at night cooking and sewing for the good of her family. She managed and handled her family possessions well by purchasing and investing in property and then selling goods to keep her husband and family safe and warm.

These are just a few biblical references of the force of wives who made things happen. Her role clearly demonstrates her unique purpose of helping her husband. She indeed is a helper designed to do what a wife is ordained to do: To help him, not to replace him or to operate outside her role or person. It is important to note that we never see the Spirit (or any of the Godhead) operating outside His design. As we mentioned earlier in this book, He is not the Father or the Son, He is the Holy Spirit, and all are one in essence. He carries out what God has ordained, and He carries it out with perfection. He is always about the work He is designed to do. He doesn't do anything of Himself. Jesus said this about the Spirit,

"Howbeit when he, the Spirit of truth, is come, He will guide you into all truth: for He shall not speak of Himself; but whatsoever He shall hear, that shall He speak and he will shew you things to come." (John 16:13)

We continue to see our omniscient God's orderliness coming through: *In the same way that God sent forth His Son in the fullness of time* (Galatians 4:4),

He sent forth "her" in the fullness of time. We see in each of these revelations of *"her"* a progression that culminates with all of the aspects of the Triune God. We see Him in the Female, Woman, Wife, and finally, in the next chapter, "Mother."

So, not only does the wife share the name helper with the Holy Spirit, in the same way, she functions like the Holy Spirit as He fills her and empowers her, if you will. She makes things happen. She helps her husband bring forth fruit, multiply, cultivate, and replenish. What an awesome role she has, to come alongside and make things happen that only she was designed to do.

Here's a beautiful story that illustrates even better the term helper. It is a word we see in I Samuel in the Old Testament that sometimes gets overlooked. The Holy Spirit pointed this word out to me as I was teaching my Titus 2 Ladies Sunday School Class a couple of years ago. It is the story of how God helped Israel win a fight against the Philistines who without his help had no chance of ever winning!

"And as Samuel was offering up the burnt offering, the Philistines drew near to battle against Israel: but the Lord thundered with a great thunder on that day upon the Philistines and discomfited them; and they were smitten before Israel. And the men of Israel went out

of Mizpeh, and pursued the Philistines, and smote them, until they came under Bethcar." (I Samuel 11:7-13)

With further study of the word, I found that in Hebrew, the meaning of the name Ebenezer is Rock or stone of help. In Hebrew, the two words that "help meet" are derived from are the words "ezer" and the word 'k'enegdo." Ezer is commonly translated as "help"

In her book "Eve and the Choice Made in Eden," Beverly Campbell explains:

"According to biblical scholar David Freedman, the Hebrew word translated there into English as "help" is ezer. This word is a combination of two roots; one meaning "to rescue," "to save," and the other meaning "to be strong." Just as the roots merged into one word, so did their meanings. At first ezer meant either "to save" or "to be strong," but in time, said Freedman, ezer "was always interpreted as 'to help,' a mixture of both nuances."

In her book, *Forgotten Women of God*, Diana Webb also clarifies this word by explaining, *"The noun "ezer" occurs 21 times in the Hebrew Bible. In eight of these instances the word means "savior." These examples are easy to identify because they are associated with other expressions of deliverance or saving.*

> *Elsewhere in the Bible, the root "ezer" means "strength.... the word is most frequently used to describe how God is an 'ezer' to man."* For example, the word "ebenezer" in 1 Samuel 7:12 is used to describe the power of God's deliverance. "Eben" means rock and "ezer" means "help" or "salvation." Ebenezer therefore means "rock of help" or "rock of salvation." So, when the battle ended in I Samuel, Samuel gave the name Ebenezer to a stone set up in recognition of God's assistance in defeating the Philistines: *"Then Samuel took a stone, and set it between Mizpeh and Shen, and called the name of it Ebenezer, saying, Hitherto hath the Lord helped us."* (I Samuel 7:12)

After studying this account in the life of Samuel and understanding the meaning behind the word Ebenezer, I could better appreciate the parallel of the word Ebenezer and the Holy Spirit. Meditating on how the Holy Spirit worked in the lives of the Israelites, reminded me of how the Holy Spirit works in our lives in times of trouble. Tying it all together, naturally I thought of the wife God created and His description of her as man's help meet. It is just another revelation of the image and likeness of God coming through again. Being created wife arguably aligns us with the third person of the Trinity. As Ebenezer represents the Lord's help for the Israelites, so does the wife, represent the Lord's help for her husband.

When God brought the woman to Adam it was clear how she would help him carry out God's work in the earth. Again, for emphasis, she would help Adam, be fruitful and multiply, she would help Adam replenish and cultivate the land that God gave them. Not only is she his helper, but she is also his strength during those times when and where God has ordained her to be. A husband and wife is no more like the image and likeness of God than when they work together to accomplish the work of God in their respective roles.

When we investigate the Word of God we see how God the Father, God the Son and God the Holy Spirit work in concert with one another to carry out the will of God. We have the greatest example we will ever need as wives to see when, where and how we can help our husbands carry out God's will. It was not God who died on the cross, it was Jesus. It was always intended for Jesus to die on the cross. It wasn't an after-thought or a change of mind on God's part. God sent Jesus and Jesus wanted to be sent.

It was the Holy Spirit who came to baptize, fill, comfort, guide, and teach men after Jesus left to be with the Father. God sent the Holy Spirit (the other comforter) and the Holy Spirit didn't argue. He always knew his role in the Godhead and as our example, wives must always stay in our place of appointment and willingly and graciously carry out the work of God as God has designed us to do. The husband is indeed the head of the woman just as God is the head of Christ (I Corinthians 11:3). My sisters, God's image and likeness is nothing to shun or reject. Remember, it is all about the *Orderliness of God!* So, wives don't think it robbery to be in submission to your own husbands. Take a moment and read I Corinthian 11.

There are many other manifestations of the image of God we see in the *wife* God created but I will leave it with you the readers to continue to explore the Godhead and discover those manifestations for yourself.

As I close this chapter and segue into the next chapter, *"He Created Her Mother,"* I want to remind you that the Spirit not only moves in, through and on us, but He also *"teaches, guides, comforts, strengthens, renews, and convicts us."* (John 16:8, 13;). So, just in case you have not noticed, the role of the wife and all those who share in God's perfect work has eternal value and in no way are inferior to any other. In our next chapter, we will see her responsibility as mother.

Notes

And God Created Her "Mother"

(Her Joint Responsibilities)

Now, for the last time, the obvious question you may be asking is, in what way do we see *"mother"* in the Godhead? Well, I'm glad you asked. Strangely enough, you might appreciate knowing that this was the most challenging chapter of all the identities for me to see the image and likeness of God. But as I continued to meditate on it, the Holy Spirit reminded me that not unlike the other identities of the *"her"* God created, the answer was in the text. So, once again the Holy Spirit led me to think on this chapter's description which I labeled: *"her joint responsibilities."* That was all it took, and once again, God's image and likeness in *Mother* was clearer than ever.

Allow me to say here that my references to mother in no way excludes those who have had the privilege of raising children they did not physically conceive, carry, or deliver out of their own wombs. Quite the contrary. Those who have had such a privilege probably identify even more because they chose to accept or step into that role of joint responsibility. So, whether you, adopt, or inherit your children through other means, all mothers' identities are rooted in the image and likeness of our Creator.

Interesting, all four *"her"* identities we have observed seem to compliment, integrate, and even overlap at points. As we continue to observe these identities of the *"her"* God created, we see yet another important connection here. As I reflected in the chapter's description, we see an inter-dependent relationship between our earthly father and mother. Therefore, there must be an inter-dependent relationship identifiable in the Godhead. For this observation I refer to it as: "the lesser to the greater." Of course, God's original design was that fathers and mothers share unique yet distinct responsibilities in raising children. Both are responsible for raising their children up in the fear and admonition of the Lord, but through their different approaches and strengths. So, with that in mind, let's first explore how our earthly fathers and mothers have a shared responsibility in raising their children.

You will recall what God told Adam and his wife Eve: *"And God blessed them, and God said unto them, be fruitful, and multiply, and replenish the earth, and subdue it: and have dominion over the fish of the sea, and over the fowl of the air, and over every living thing that moveth upon the earth."* (Genesis 1:28)

So, one of the first joint responsibilities we see that a mother has with her husband is to be fruitful and multiply, as in bear children. Children cannot be born apart from this joint activity, although, each makes a unique contribution to this miraculous activity. Again, it is clear that a mother's role and responsibility in raising her children is definitely seen in the Godhead as well. A mother has been physiologically and biologically designed to fulfill her part of the child's rearing. This joint responsibility is pleasing to God because it reflects His likeness. The parents are like the Godhead who jointly work together to bring salvation to all men. The mother's work includes but not limited to attributes that supply all the nourishment necessary for the health of the child from the womb until and even after delivery. The Father's seed that is planted inside the womb is essential to the conception of the child and his godly guidance and discipline is required in raising up of a child in the way he or she should go. And of course, the mother's ability to nurture the soul and spirit of the child is an illustration of joint responsibilities in her role as mother. It is the same idea we see in the Godhead.

We saw all the Godhead in action in the creation of man and we continue to see the Godhead in action in our spiritual birth as well. From the will of the Father who loved the world so much that He sent His only begotten Son into the world to die on the cross, to the raising up of the same by the Holy Spirit. John 3:16&17; Romans 8:11; I Corinthians 15:3&4.

In the same way, the birth, the raising, and the nurturing are all a part of God's design for the mother. I believe most mothers will agree that there is nothing like the experience of carrying a child for nine months (more or less), the labor pains she endures before delivery, and finally, the joy of giving birth to a child who is totally dependent on her for everything. Isn't that just like our Triune God? Even the imagery we see in the earthly parental responsibilities is so much like the Godhead. We can see all the Godhead hands-on deck when a person is "born again". And in the same way, all hands are on deck when a mother brings a child into the world. Although the father's role is quite different at childbirth, he is none the less just as important to the process as that child comes into a household where two parents await their arrival with joy and excitement. Waiting to provide all that child needs and receive all that child brings into the relationship.

At salvation, newborn babes arrive with the need of God the Father, God the Son, and God the Holy Spirit. Scripture is clear that the responsibility for the child is a shared work of the Godhead. Jesus is the way to salvation, the Fathers draws his Elect to Salvation, and the Holy Spirit quickens and makes alive a babe in Christ.

As the babe grows, the Spirit washes, fills, and teaches the babe how to live a holy and sanctified life. As well, the Son Jesus Christ sits at the right-hand making intercessions for the child to His Father. Jesus's blood continues to *cleanse the believer from all unrighteousness, and He will present us faultless before the throne. (I John 3:15, Jude 24).*

Just as in the physical birth of a child, the child arrives with a natural desire for milk. And so it is with the newborn babe.; they too desire the sincere milk of the Word that they may grow. Both the mother and the Spirit of God are ready to feed their children.

Other joint responsibilities we see at work in the Godhead is a God who defends, protects, and fights for His children in times of trouble. We see the Lord of Hosts preparing a place for his children to be with him throughout all eternity. He who loves his children with a love that can never be separated (Romans 8:38-39).

These are the same joint responsibilities we see in the mother sharing with her husband. Mothers have the awesome joint responsibility of washing our children both physically and spiritually. Like Jesus, moms are always at the throne of God making and pleading for God to not only save our children but to keep our children safe from all alarms as the song goes. Mothers are natural lovers of their children. When a child needs to be comforted, more times than not, that child looks to their mother for comfort! No one can comfort the heart of a son or daughter the way a mother can comfort them. When a mother comforts, she comforts with the intent of easing the pain of her child. A mother's ability to soothe, comfort and console her children is so like the Godhead. She will stay up late and rise early to ensure her children are well cared for. When sickness overtakes her child, she will assume the role of a primary caregiver at her own health's expense. In other words, she sacrifices all for her children. Mothers like the fathers are commanded to *train our children up in the way they should go... (Proverbs 22:6).* She spends most of her time counseling and training her children in sometime unique ways that only a mother would think about.

And last, just like our heavenly Father, the safety of a child is first and foremost on her mind and there is nothing she would not do to protect them from danger. I think you will agree with me that motherly instinct is rooted in God's image and likeness! Only when there are physical or emotional compromises of a mother's mental capacity will she not seek to protect her child from danger. No other creature is willing or capable of protecting a mother's child equal to herself. She possesses a love that operates on automatic! Do you remember this account of the two women in I Kings 3:22-27?

[22] "No!" the other woman shouted. "He was your son. My baby is alive!" "The dead baby is yours," the first woman yelled. "Mine is alive!" They argued back and forth in front of Solomon, [23] until finally he said, "Both of you say this live baby is yours. [24] Someone bring me a sword." A sword was brought, and Solomon ordered, [25] "Cut the baby in half! That way each of you can have part of him." [26] "Please don't kill my son," the baby's mother screamed. "Your Majesty, I love him very much, but give him to her. Just don't kill him." The other woman shouted, "Go ahead and cut him in half. Then neither of us will have the baby." [27] Solomon said, "Don't kill the baby." Then he pointed to the first woman, "She is his real mother. Give the baby to her."

Now compare that account to the many assurances of God's protection for us throughout the scriptures:

You are my hiding place; you will protect

me from trouble and surround me with songs of deliverance.
Psalm 32:7

God is our refuge and strength, an ever-present help in trouble.
Psalm 46:1

Be strong and courageous. Do not be afraid or terrified because of them, for the Lord your God goes with you; he will never leave you nor forsake you.
Deuteronomy 31:6

You make your saving help my shield, and your right hand sustains me; your help has made me great. You provide a broad path for my feet, so that my ankles do not give way.
Psalm 18:35-36

The Lord will fight for you; you need only to be still.
Exodus 14:14

As I wrap up this chapter on the *"mother"* God created, I will conclude by saying, you don't have to look long at a mother to see the image and likeness of God. But it blew my mind once when I was preparing for a weekly radio program and I stumbled upon this verse: *As one whom his mother comforteth, so will I comfort you; and ye shall be comforted in Jerusalem. (Isaiah 66:13 KJV).*

Can you believe that? Almighty God who created mothers, says His love is like hers! In essence, Did God just say, "I like what I see in the mother I created?" WOW!! Now that's truly an interesting *"Lesser to the Greater" observation.* I pray you are like me and want to be a mother after God's own heart.

"Mother"

Notes

Conclusion

First, I pray by now you have sensed my excitement about being created in God's image and likeness as well as my appreciation for God's order. And yet ladies, I am not oblivious to the fact that it's no longer a big thing for women to live comfortably outside God's design. But please know it is this author's prayer that as we meditate on each of the *"Hers"* God created that it would lead us back to Titus 2:3-5. A mandate that will truly make the difference in our next generation of women and bring back glory to God, our Creator, as He intended.

Last, as you reflect on these observations, you may be asking the same question Pastor Steven J. Lawson was asked after preaching a very powerful message. As I remember the story, a gentleman from the audience, as many often do, was moved to shake Pastor Steve's hand, and politely thank him for the message. But what followed his thank-you was a very sobering and unexpected question: *"So what?"* To say the least, whenever I hear Pastor Lawson speak, I remember that question or better yet when I speak or teach.

Dr., Lawson's story reminds me of a sobering declaration written by the wisest man that ever lived, King Solomon. Seemingly, King Solomon, also called "the Preacher," contemplated a similar question as he ended his book of Ecclesiastes. He closed with these words: *Let us hear the conclusion of the whole matter. (Ecclesiastes 12:13).*

Like King Solomon, I think it fitting to end this book, with all its observations, unveilings, and sometimes mild interpretations, with my own sobering conclusion of this whole matter. Conclusions can be very helpful especially after reading through someone else's personal experiences and revealed scripture discoveries. So, after reading *And God Created Her,* you too may possibly be thinking *"So what?"* So, I conclude by addressing the comment, *"So what?"*

Just a quick glimpse back at the "Introduction" (I promise I will not repeat the whole chapter). I want to quickly tie the introduction to the conclusion because both are right on point to address the *"So what?"*

The key point I wanted to convey right from the beginning in my introduction all the way through the final chapter was this, *God is a God of order,* so I shared my coined phrase: *"The Orderliness of God."* You will recall in the introduction that

Conclusion

my coined phrase was a revelation by the Holy Spirit during my personal worship/Bible Study Time *(with respect to literary rights, I request that my readers and fellow authors respectfully quote the author when referencing this phrase.)*

It is no light matter that God is a God of Order. And the woman being made in God's image and likeness, in the same way, is no light matter. The *Orderliness of God* is paramount to our Christian walk. It is His image and likeness that shines in darkness; it really does light up the world.

The *Orderliness of God* I focused on in this book is not just a historical fact or a one-time observation of God; quite the contrary! To accurately grasp the *Orderliness of God* is to take to heart all that preceded and continues to follow that Trinitarian Portrait of God and Man (Woman). WOW! Please don't miss that. An eternal Trinitarian Portrait.

God gave man His image and likeness at creation. That image and likeness reflected the Trinity on earth that existed in the Godhead. Unfortunately, man fell! That image and likeness was marred. But then, in the fullness of time, God the Son, took upon himself the form of that man that he created in His own image and likeness, and perfectly walked out that image and likeness before man. Do you see the continuous order of God at work in His relationship with the man He created? And yet, it was that perfect walk that took the Godman to His crucifixion and ultimately to His grave. Determined to redeem that marred image and likeness that He created, Jesus was resurrected from the grave and man was restored to reflect that Trinitarian Portrait on earth once again.

What you have read in this book can either be lightly received or it will cause you to go deeper in your meditation of what it means for a woman to live out the image and likeness of God in today's culture. It is your choice. I promise, that if you go deeper and meditate on our unique and glorious identity, you will not walk or make decisions the same way. I am certain that you will be more aware and intentional about your walk and prayerful about your decisions.

Unfortunately, we still see the marring of God's image and likeness in today's women, even Christian women. As I alluded to earlier, there seems to be no thought of consequences for our love and practice of worldly images and likenesses. Too many times, the new un-God-like lifestyles are written off as being "in style" and "normal" for today. The common mindset is that it really doesn't matter to God how we look, think, or act. It's what's in our heart that counts. Not realizing that your heart is being exposed by the ugly things we say, think, and do. Surprise! *"As a man thinketh in his heart so is he."* (Proverbs 23:7). You are living out what's in your heart. This ugly marring of God's image and likeness in our hearts exposes and reveals our ugly attitude toward God. And what is notable is that God, *"The Very God"* continues to allow such disdain to be attached to His image and likeness. But of course, that speaks to the long suffering and mercy of God, *her* Creator. The apostle Peter reminds us that God is not slack concerning his promise as some men count slackness but is long suffering toward us, not willing that any should perish but that all should come to repentance! (II Peter 3:7)

R. C. Sproul mentioned in one of his audio messages on the holiness of God, entitled the *Otherness of God,* that one of the central messages from the 16th Century was that the quest of the Christian life was to live Coram Deo, which means before the face of God. Sproul further added what that meant was, "that all of our life is to be lived with an awareness that we are living in His presence and that we are living under His authority."[3]

I completely agree and I would humbly add that in the deepest sense that this phrase, the "Orderliness of God," goes even further to say that we are not just living with the awareness of His presence but that we ARE His presence! Carrying about in our body is the presence of the Trinity. Reflecting His image and likeness all over the world. The thought that God's image and likeness was etched in mankind at creation would prayerfully awaken in us a determination to glorify Him like we never have before. Realizing that this image and likeness is an eternal presence and reflection that promises to materialize in a perfect body in the life that is to come.

Just think, we are experiencing a preview of what is to come as written in I John 3:2. *Beloved, now are we the sons of God, and it doth not yet appear what we shall be: but we know that, when he shall appear, we shall be like him; for we shall see him as he is.*

My *"So what?"* conclusion is, Let's live like we were created in the image and likeness of God!

---

[3] https://www.youtube.com/watch?v=_Dm_wj0bPsw

About the Author

Rosalyn and husband Gary have been married only to one another since November 1974. They have one Son, Quincy Pernell, and two grandsons, Mason Pernell and Peyton Jaxson Hickman. In addition to serving her husband, Rosalyn also serves as the Executive Director of Covenant Keypers, Inc. (www.covenantkeypers.org) founded by her and her husband in 2005.

Saved at the age of ten on Cooley Street in Chattanooga, TN, Rosalyn now mentors, counsels, and disciples young women throughout the southeast. She also speaks at women's conferences, retreats, workshops, and seminars. She uses her Bible study and prayer group platforms to disciple young women and launch one-on-one up close and personal relationships.

In 2014, Rosalyn released her first book *Anybody Home? In Search of the Titus Woman.* She wrote the book to encourage wives who can feasibly afford to be home with their children to explore the advantages of being there and to pursue the role of the Titus 2 Woman that God created her to be. Since the COVID Pandemic, she also continues to reach out to women through YouTube videos and other virtual platforms.

Rosalyn earned her Bachelor of Science degree in Business Administration from Tennessee Wesleyan College in Athens, TN, and her Master of Science degree in Christian Psychological Studies from Richmont Graduate University, Atlanta, GA (Chattanooga, TN campus).

She also holds certifications as a Marriage Coach, Life Innovations Prepare/Enrich Marriage Administrator, and a Prepare/Enrich Seminar Director/Trainer.

Rosalyn loves to pray, serve in her home with her husband, by hosting missionaries, married couples, and individuals in their home for overnight rest and relaxation.

She is a member of Resurrected Reformed Baptist Church in Chattanooga, TN, Eddie D. Jacks, Pastor. She serves as one of the teachers of the Women's Sunday School Class, Missionary Coordinator, and alongside her husband, serves as the primary Marriage Ministry leaders.

For any of your speaking, teaching, or counseling needs, contact Mrs. Hickman at gbooksnme@gmail.com.

Join us for Covenant Keypers' events at www.covenantkeypers.org

www.ingramcontent.com/pod-product-compliance
Lightning Source LLC
Chambersburg PA
CBHW070648050426
42451CB00008B/315